I0191210

GOSPEL OF CHRIST

Jacob

GOSPEL OF CHRIST

God became human. Jesus Christ, the Wise Teacher, the Holy Doctor, the Prince of Peace, the Son of God, the Sage, Light, came into the world and redeemed the world. Jesus Christ, God's covenant incarnate, the earthly projection of a beginningless, endless, omnipresent Being. Jesus Christ is God and is humanity, the ultimate symbol, the living sign of the two natures in human beings, the human and the divine, in synthesis. This is the way to enlightenment, to becoming a true and living being. The Incarnation shows us that the divine world coexists within each human being. This world, this life, this mind, this earth are holy and beautiful and have been redeemed.

Mary, the mother of Jesus, was engaged to be married to a man named Joseph when she became pregnant by the Holy Spirit. Joseph, being just, did not want to publicly humiliate Mary and so chose to break their engagement privately.

While Joseph thought about these matters God came to him in a dream. 'Joseph, do not be afraid to take Mary as your wife because the baby within her is of the Sacred Spirit. She will give birth to a boy and you will name him Jesus, meaning God's redeemer, and Emmanuel, meaning God is with us.'

The Emperor Caeser Augustus issued a decree that all the people of the Empire would be counted and taxed. All people went to their hometowns in order to be counted in this census. Joseph and Mary travelled from their home in Nazareth to the city of Bethlehem, where Joseph's family had originated. In Bethlehem Mary delivered her firstborn son in a stable because there were no rooms in the city.

In the fields nearby were shepherds keeping watch over their sheep and goats. Heaven opened to them and the light of God shone and they were scared. The shepherds were then at peace. Heaven was filled with praise and song: 'Good and joyful news is brought to you and to all people. Today in Bethlehem a Savior is born. Jesus Christ. Go and find him lying in a manger. Glory to God in the highest and peace and good will to all those on earth.'

The shepherds went to Bethlehem and found Mary, Joseph, and the baby in a stable. The shepherds glorified and praised God and told the story to many others.

Joseph and Jesus spent many hours together, working in Joseph's carpentry shop. Jesus increased in wisdom and stature, and drew close to God.

In the fifteenth year of the reign of Tiberius Caesar a messenger was sent out before Jesus to prepare the way. The voice of one crying in the wilderness: "Prepare the way of the Lord, make his paths straight." John the Baptist preached in the wilderness of Judea, saying, "Repent because the kingdom of the sky is near."

Many came to be baptized by him in the Jordan River, to be cleansed of their sins. "I baptize with water but one is coming who is mighty, and he will baptize with the Holy Spirit and with fire."

Jesus came to the Jordan to be baptized by John. John said, "It is I who should be baptized by you."

Jesus responded, "It is right that you should baptize me so that all may be fulfilled."

When Jesus was baptized and came out of the water the heavens opened and the Sacred Spirit of God descended on Jesus as a dove. A voice from the sky spoke, 'This is my son, whom I love.'

The Spirit then drove Jesus into the wilderness. He was there for forty days, fasting. In nature he searched for harmony, and to be with the power within all things. He lit candles and incense and prayed and drew close to God. Jesus experienced the sacredness of existence and a deep-seated respect and a unity with all. He opened, like a flower, to the great mystery, the Sacred Spirit.

The tempter came to Jesus and said, 'If you are the Son of God command these stones to become bread.'

Jesus answered, "Man shall not live by bread alone but by the word of God."

Then the devil took Jesus into Jerusalem to the roof of the temple and said, 'If you are the Son of God jump and the angels will bear you up and you will not be hurt.'

Jesus responded, "I will not tempt God."

The devil then took Jesus up to a high mountain and showed him all the kingdoms of the world, and their glory and power. The devil said, 'All these things, this power, I will give to you for they are in my command and in the command of whomever I choose. Only fall down and worship me.'

Jesus replied, "I will worship only God and serve only God. I forgive even you Satan. Now be gone."

Then the devil left and the Spirit of God came to help Jesus.

Before his baptism Jesus had been a boy and when Jesus returned from the desert he was a man, prepared to begin his work.

When Jesus heard that John had been imprisoned he left Nazareth and travelled to Capernaum by the sea.

Jesus began to preach, saying, "Repent because the Kingdom of Heaven is here. Now. The people who have lived in darkness have seen a great light, and to those who have been dead life is given." Jesus taught in the synagogues and became famous in the region.

As Jesus travelled by the Sea of Galilee people pressed in on him. On the shore were fishing boats. Jesus went to one where Simon was mending his nets. Jesus asked Simon if a boat could be pushed out a little ways from the land so that he could speak from the boat and not be pressed by the crowds.

Simon and his brother Andrew were both disciples of John. They knew Jesus was the man whom John had told them of, saying, "He is the lamb of God which takes away the sin of the world. I saw the Spirit of God descend on him. I baptize with water but he baptizes with the Spirit. This is the Son of God."

Andrew went to Jesus and Jesus asked him, "What do you seek?"

Andrew answered, "To know where you live, Teacher."

And Jesus said, "Come and see."

Andrew followed Jesus to his house and stayed with him that day. Andrew then went to his brother Simon and told him, "I have found the Messiah, the Christ." He brought Simon to Jesus.

To Simon Jesus said, "You are Simon the son of Jonah. You shall be called Peter, the Stone."

Andrew and Peter left their nets to follow Jesus. A little later the brothers James and John, who were also fishermen, came to follow Jesus.

There was a wedding in Cana at which Jesus was to minister. He came with his brothers and his mother Mary. When the wine at the party ran out Jesus told the workers to fill six stone water pots with water. "Now fill a glass from a pot and serve it to the guest of honor."

When the guest of honor tasted the drink he said loudly to the groom, "You have kept the best wine for last."

After the wedding Jesus, Mary, and his brothers traveled to Capernaum.

Jesus went up onto a mountain and prayed all night. The next day he called the twelve disciples to gather with him. These were his disciples: Peter, Andrew his brother, the brothers James and John, Philip, Bartholomew, Thomas, Matthew, Simon the Patriot, Judas Iscariot, Thaddeus, and James. They were ordained his apostles.

There were women with Jesus: Martha, Mary Magdalene, who had been cured of seven demons, Joanna, the wife of the steward of Herod tetrarch of Galilee, and Susanna, and many others.

Jesus travelled Galilee, teaching in the synagogues about the Kingdom of the Spirit of God and healing the people's sickness and disease. His fame spread through Israel and Syria, and people came to Jesus to hear him and touch him and to follow him.

When multitudes had gathered Jesus went up on a mountain with his disciples and sat and began to teach:

"Blessed are those who know that they are lacking in spirit. Blessed are those who live with less. Blessed are those who have had troubles. Blessed are those who don't put themselves above others. Blessed are those who know this world is lacking in justice. Blessed are those who know compassion for others. Blessed are those who feel pure love. Blessed are those who seek peace. Blessed are those who strive for justice even when persecuted and hated and attacked and imprisoned. A joyful life is theirs. They will know God. Blessed are those who are thankful and, if even for a moment, see the beauty of life.

You are the salt of the earth. You are the light of the world, as a city on a hill, unable to hide. One does not light a candle and put it under a basket, but on a stand so that it may give light to all in the house. Let your light shine so that others may see your goodness, and glorify God.

Treat children with love and care, and raise your children with respect, as you respect your parents and elders. This world knows such sadness and cruelty. Why should the children be hurt? Whoever would hurt a child, it would be better if he were drowned.

The one who offends hurts himself and cuts himself off from God, as drowning in the cold dark ocean, or as burning in unquenchable fire, or as being eaten from within by worms.

Have peace, one with another. Cling to the goodness within yourself and nurture it, for if it disappears, despair.

If your brother offends you, speak to him about it. And forgive him. And if he offends you seven times in a day, forgive him. How many times should you forgive him? Always.

When you pray, forgive, and God will forgive you. You won't be arrested if you get angry at your brother and call him a fool, or weak, or worthless. But you'll still be judged. You have so many gifts to give, but first you must make peace with others. And make peace with your adversary before things get out of hand and there is violence or you are jailed. And you must also learn to be forgiven. Search your soul and make amends for sins. Pray for the forgiveness of sins. Ask for forgiveness from others. You must find a constructive attitude towards trouble and must learn to forgive the past. It is peace I have come to bring.

I have not come to destroy the law nor the teachings of the prophets, but to fulfill them. Live not by the law, but by the Spirit. Know tolerance, receptiveness, adaptability, and moderation. Do not be angry and hateful when another does not live by the principles that you do. But strive for the good. Only your righteousness will bring you to God. If a man calls you a fool on your spiritual journey, know that he is on his spiritual journey as well.

Do not judge others so that you yourself won't be judged by the same measure. Why do you carry on about the speck in your brother's eye, offering to remove it, and ignore the boulder in your own eye? First remove that boulder from your own eye and then you'll be able to see clearly to remove the speck from your brother's eye. The blind cannot lead the blind, or both will fall into a ditch. And the disciple must first learn from the master in order to become a master.

You have heard 'an eye for an eye and a tooth for a tooth,' but now I say 'do not take revenge.' If you are hit on the right cheek turn and give the other cheek. And if someone sues you and takes your coat, give him your sweater too. And if you are forced by one of the occupation troops to carry his gear a mile, walk with him two miles. If someone wants to borrow from you, lend. If someone asks you for something, give it.

All people love and respect those who love them in return, their close family and friends. This isn't new. But I'll sing a new song: have love and compassion for all. Treat others the same as you'd like others to treat you. Make all men your brothers and all women your sisters.

You have heard 'love your neighbor and hate your enemy.' But now I say, 'love your enemy, do good to those who hate you, pray for those who use and persecute and hurt you.' And you say, 'where is the justice in this?' You be good, that is justice. In this way you will be of God, because God's sun shines on evil and goodness alike, and God's rain falls on the just and unjust alike.

Seek understanding. Ask and you will receive, seek and you will find, knock and the door will be opened to you. If your child asks for bread, you don't give him a stone. And if he asks for a fish, do you give him a snake? God also gives good gifts.

Pray simply with simple words. Language is often inadequate for communion with God. Then use silence. God does not need the words but that they bring you closer to God.

Do not make a big public show out of your prayers, but go to a quiet place, such as a closet, and shut the door.

Find peace of mind, a stillness, a harmony with all, a receptiveness. Quiet the demons of the mind, the chaos. Sweep away the dust of the mind, the illusions, and elevate your awareness. Through peace one communes with the sacred power of existence. In prayer one may be liberated, find truth, find completeness, be open to and overcome by the Sacred Spirit. Empty the mind and let God fill it. When you pray say,

'Our Sacred Father,

Our Holy Spirit,

I yearn for you, and for your goodness.

You are my life, and the life of all the world.

I forgive others, and know that I am forgiven.

You are the Kingdom, the power, the glory forever.

Amen.'

Meditation, prayer, enlightenment, God, Heaven, the Sacred Spirit, the truth, are all inseparable.

Simply do what you say you will do and respect the bonds you make before God, in particular the bond between husband and wife. Marriage is in the heart. Honesty is purity before God. You must strive to be true and then you will be truly alive. Your trustworthiness will be your bond.

Seek to know the spirits of others, not simply their flesh.

Some cannot take a spouse because of physical reasons, or because they have chosen not to for the sake of God. This requires tolerance.

Do not justify your actions before men. What is esteemed by God you must find within. And how can a man be justified before others? John the Baptist came, fasting and refusing wine, and people said he had a demon. I feast and drink and people say I am a glutton and a friend of sinners. You must be true to a higher law.

Don't make a big show out of giving to the poor, but do it secretly. Don't give so that you may be glorified.

When you fast do it for yourself and for God, not for others. Wash when you fast and don't make a big show of it.

A man's life is so much more than his possessions. Don't build up treasure which you must always be worried about. Where your treasure is, that's also where your heart is. So sell what you have and do good with the money. Save up treasure in the spiritual world, which you may have in abundance.

So many are always looking ahead, knowing that if they can only obtain their next goal then all in their lives will be happiness. But death steals in all too soon.

No one can serve two masters because he will hate one master and love the other. You cannot serve both God and money. So do not worry about food, or drink, or clothes.

Look at the birds. They don't work, yet they are fed and housed. And why worry about clothes? Look at the flowers of the field, how they grow. They don't work. Even the kings of this world are not dressed as beautifully as these flowers.

God will provide. It is the Godless who strive for riches. Strive for God and for righteousness. Do not worry about tomorrow because tomorrow will take care of itself.

It is easy to take the wide, busy streets. But the path of life is narrow and difficult to find. The path may be known if God is known, because God is true reality.

Many who are last in society are first in the Kingdom of Heaven, where the prophets are. Many who are first in society are not with God. Saying, 'Lord, Lord' does not open the door to Heaven, but doing God's work does.

Your eyes are like windows. If all you see is evil in the world then you will be filled with darkness. If you see goodness then you will be filled with light. And if you have no light within you, your world is so dark. But if you are filled with light, you will be the light of the world.

You must reap what you sow. If you plant corruption your fruit will be thorns and thistles. A good tree brings forth good fruit, as a good person brings forth the goodness from the treasure of their heart. A person cannot hide what is in their heart."

When Jesus finished the people were amazed because of the authority with which he had spoken. Thousands followed as Jesus came down from the mountain.

A leper approached Jesus saying, "Please, I know you can heal me, if you want to."

Jesus, moved with compassion, touched the man, saying, "I do want to." And the man's leprosy was healed. "Go to the temple and offer a gift in thanks."

Jesus was unable to enter Capernaum openly because of the crowds that would gather. So he stayed out in desolate wilderness, and prayed, and soon people from all over came to be with him.

Jesus went into Capernaum with his disciples on the holy day and entered the house of worship to teach. There in the synagogue was a crazed man crying, "Leave us alone. You have come to destroy us. I know who you are."

And Jesus said, "Have peace and come out of him."

A dark spirit tore the man and threw him and cried with a loud voice and came out of him. All were amazed and asked each other, "What new doctrine is this? Who is this man that he can heal like this?"

Jesus then spoke, "As this man was filled with a demon so too is this world. There is a beast which will be driven out of this world. Its name is Satan. There is a battle raging within, and peace will come."

Then Jesus saw a sick woman who had been bed-ridden for a long time. He said to her, "You are freed from your illness." He laid his hands on her and her body became straight and strong and she glorified God.

A teacher of the law, seeing this, was indignant and said aloud, "There are six days of the week for doing work, so heal on those days, not on the holy day."

Jesus answered, "Don't you take your donkey out of its stall and lead it to water on the holy day? Shouldn't this woman who has been tied up by illness for eighteen years also be freed?"

There was a man with an ill-formed hand there. Jesus then asked the teacher of the law, "If you had one sheep and it fell into a ravine on the holy day, would you rescue it? Yes. Is a man not as worthy of help as a sheep? Is it legal to do good on the Sabbath?" The teacher held his peace. Jesus was sad because of the hardness of his heart.

Jesus turned to the man with the deformed hand. "Stretch out your hand." The man stretched out his hand and it was restored.

The teacher of the law left angrily.

After attending services Jesus, James, and John entered the house of Peter and Andrew. Peter's mother-in-law lay sick with fever. Jesus took her hand and lifted her up and the fever left her. She rose out of bed.

In the evening as the sun was setting many gathered at the door and many who were sick with disease and mental illness were brought to him and he healed them all. Jesus took the people's infirmities and bore their sicknesses. And the devils he cast out knew him as Christ as he knew them.

In the morning, rising long before the sun, Jesus went out to a solitary place to pray. Peter, Andrew, James, and John, not knowing why he had left, followed after him. When they found him they told him that everyone was looking for him.

Jesus replied, "Let us travel to a new town to preach. The Kingdom is for all those who seek it."

Jesus was invited into the house of two sisters, Martha and Mary, who lived in Bethany. While Mary sat and listened to Jesus, Martha was busy cooking and serving.

Martha asked Jesus, "What do you think of my sister who sits there while I work? Shouldn't she help me?"

"Martha, to provide such hospitality is a beautiful thing. Peace be with you. You are troubled by so many things. Mary has chosen to sit and talk with me, and she has chosen well."

That evening Jesus asked his disciples to procure a boat so that they could cross the Sea of Galilee. A boat was found and launched, Jesus and his disciples on board. A strong storm began, the waves pounding the boat, breaking over the gunwale and filling the boat, and the hull sounding as though it would crack. Jesus was asleep. His disciples woke him, saying, "Save us. Don't you care that we're all going to die?"

Jesus replied, "Why are you so afraid? Have faith." He stood and said, "Peace." The sea and the wind stilled and all was calm.

The others were amazed, asking each other, "What kind of man is this that even the water and wind obey him?"

Then Jesus spoke, "I have come to bring peace to the world. So do not set all against its opposite, death against life. Do not turn all into war. Do not say this is good therefore that is bad, this is right therefore that is wrong. The truth often lies between the extremes. I do not want violence, not even in the heart or mind, but patience and endurance. The war is within. Though many exist they all exist within one."

When they had crossed the sea they were in the region of Dekapolis. There, in the hills above the shore, was a man who cried down to Jesus, "I don't want you here, Son of God. You're here to torture me." The man had lived in the tombs there in the hills for many years, naked, crying, and cutting himself with stones. Many times people had come out to try to control him and had tied him, but every time he had become fierce and had broken free.

Jesus went to the man and asked him, "What is your name?"

The man answered, "My name is Legion, because we are many." Within the man lived many petty spirits: greed, hatred and anger, selfishness and arrogance, delusion and falsehood, and many more. Jesus said to the spirits, "Go," and they came out of the man and entered a herd of pigs nearby. The pigs became violent and rushed off a steep embankment into the sea, drowning in the water.

Jesus then said, "An animal could not live one hour with the horrors in its mind that man endures."

The man who had been possessed was now in his right mind. Clothes were given to him and he sat quietly. The man asked Jesus if he could travel with him, but Jesus told the man, "Go home to your friends and tell them of the great things the God of compassion has done for you." And the man departed.

After crossing back to Capernaum by boat, Jesus was in his house. Word that he had returned spread. After a few days a crowd had formed at the house, filling it and spreading into the road.

A group carrying a stretcher, on which was a man unable to move, approached the house, but was unable to enter due to the crowds. Lifting the stretcher above their heads they made their way slowly into the house.

Jesus, on seeing the faith of those who had carried the sick man, said to the man, "Son, be full of joy, because your sins are forgiven."

Teachers of the law were there in the house and when they heard Jesus' words thought to themselves, 'This man is a blasphemer. Only God can forgive sins.'

Jesus felt their thoughts and said to them, "Why have evil in your hearts? Humans on earth can forgive sins and can heal." Then, turning to the sick man, said, "Arise, pick up your cot, and walk."

And the man stood and glorified God and left to his house. When the crowd saw this they were in awe at the glory of God and at the fact that humans could have such power.

A small group of friends brought a blind man to Jesus. They asked Jesus to touch and heal their friend. Jesus took the man by the hand and led him away from the others and asked him, "Do you believe that I am able to give you sight?" The man replied that he did. Jesus then touched his eyes and his eyes were opened.

While Jesus was speaking to the man a nobleman, a ruling official, came and said, "My daughter is dying. She is only twelve years old and is too young to die. Please, come sir, or my child will die."

Jesus followed the nobleman to his house. On the way, in the crowded streets, many pressed around Jesus. A woman came behind him and touched him. She had bled for twelve years and had spent all of her money on physicians, but though she had suffered by them, she was no better, but the bleeding grew worse. She had told herself that all she needed to do was touch Jesus and she would be healed.

Jesus turned and said to her, "Daughter, be comforted." And the bleeding stopped and the woman felt the healing within.

When Jesus came into the nobleman's house he knew the girl was dead because her mother and others mourned. Jesus said to them, "The girl isn't dead, but is sleeping." He went into the girl's bedroom and took her by the hand and her spirit came again and she rose. Jesus called for food to be brought to the girl.

The official then said to Jesus, "Thank you. And how may I be righteous in the eyes of the Lord?"

"You are a ruler, so rule well. You must first master yourself before you can master others. You must perform your duties by treating others right. You must deal with people equally and serve the interests of the community. And you must always keep justice in mind."

A man came to Jesus and asked him, "What should I do to be with God?"

Jesus replied, "Do not murder, do not commit adultery, do not steal, do not bear false witness, honor your parents."

The man replied, "I have kept these commandments, but still I feel lacking."

"Then love others as you love yourself. Go and sell all that you have and give to those in need and come and follow in my way."

The man went away sad because he was very rich.

Then Jesus said to his disciples, "It is easier for a camel to go through the eye of a needle than for a rich man to be Messiah."

Peter then said, "I have given up my possessions and have followed you. What have I earned?"

Jesus replied, "You who have followed in the way of God and have forsaken riches and have found humility are alive, whole, and complete, and have all the world and are with God."

Simon the Patriot asked Jesus, "Teacher, what must I do to be perfect?"

Jesus responded, "What is perfection? Without failure you would not be fully alive and you would not know humility."

"Then is there anything I must do?"

"First devote yourself to God's path. Open your mind, your existence, and rise above the smallness of your relative viewpoint. Seek true understanding. Seek your own true nature. Seek to free your mind. Be open to the power within all things which is God. Be awake to God, and to God's balance. Then you will know awe and wonder, and will realize your Godhood, your being with God. Then you will truly serve the world."

Bartholomew asked Jesus, "Teacher, tell us about God."

Jesus responded, "God is ultimately indescribable. God is to be worshipped and adored. God is beginningless and endless. God is life-giving energy, the transcendent power of creation and governance, truth and order. The infinite, immanent, absolute reality which is the divine ground of time, space, and being. God is the source and essence, the flow and sustaining power, of the Universe. The unfolding continuation of all. God is our Father, our Mother, the Holy One, a holy sage, a mountain, light, the dove and the crane, the lamb and the lion, and many powerful symbols. God is the great mystery of existence. God is existence. God is all that one is, and the fact that anything is. God is the sacred. God is the ultimate question and the ultimate answer. God is wonder and true understanding. God is true being. God is communion."

Bartholomew was confused. "So you say God is all things, then is there no sin in the world? No evil?"

Jesus answered, "All the universe is sacred, though certainly there is evil. By holding a deep-seated respect for existence one may see the evil, the beast, eating away at the world, devouring the sacred."

Jesus was walking by fields of grain on the holy day. He was hungry and picked some grain to eat.

Some teachers of the law saw this and said to Jesus, "It's not legal to reap on the holy day."

Jesus replied, "Haven't you read that King David and his men entered God's temple and ate the bread offered on the altar, food only the priests could legally eat? The law says that on the holy day ministers profane the temple by working but are blameless. This world is God's temple and humans are the priests of God's worship. The Sabbath was made for humanity, not humanity for the Sabbath. Stop your blaming and condemning. The holy day is a day of rest, so be at peace. Go and practice compassion, decency, and empathy. Do you see no good? God is here with you, now."

One said to Jesus, "Master, we want to see a sign, a miracle from Heaven."

Jesus sighed deeply in his spirit and said, "When you look at the clouds you know whether or not there'll be rain, and when the sky is clear in the winter you know the night will be cold, and when you feel the wind come from the

South you know it will be hot. You can discern the signs of the sky, but not the signs of the times. You seek a sign? I am the Living Sign. You seek a miracle? Do you not know of the miracle in the womb? Or of the miracle of the stars and the many worlds on which there is life? Do you not see the miracle of existence all around? The miracle of the mountains, and oceans, and of love? God is miracle."

Jesus travelled to Nazareth, the place of his childhood. He went to the grave of his father Joseph and spoke with him.

Later he went to the house of worship and began to teach. Those who heard him were amazed at his wisdom. Those who witnessed Jesus healing the sick were amazed at his works. But many began to say, "Isn't this the carpenter's son? Isn't Mary his mother? Isn't James his brother?" They saw Jesus as a pretender and as self-important.

Jesus said, "No prophet is accepted in his own country nor honored in his own house."

Herod the tetrarch had John the Baptist beheaded. John's disciples came and took the body and buried it, then went and told Jesus.

Herod heard of all that Jesus had done and the stories being told about him, that he was one of the old prophets risen again, or John the Baptist. Herod said to himself, 'I have beheaded John the Baptist. Now I must learn more about this man.'

When Jesus heard of John the Baptist's death he went off to the Sea of Galilee and went up to a mountain, into the wilderness to sit and be alone and to pray.

Many people, from all over, about five thousand men, women, and children, followed, bringing paraplegics, the blind, those who couldn't talk, those hurt in accidents, and many others. They had heard what great things Jesus had done. Jesus was moved by compassion towards them. Jesus healed many and many more pressed in on him to touch him. Some fell, crying, "You are the Son of God."

A deaf man was brought to Jesus. Jesus held the man's ears and, looking up to the sky, said, "Be opened." And the man could hear. The people saw this and glorified God.

Jesus began to speak. "If a person purges evil spirits from his soul, those destructive demons will try to later return to their old home in the heart. The evil will be stronger and the person will be worse off than when he began. But if those spirits are done away with a second time, then that man is the strongest.

A man went out to the fields to sow. As he threw the seed some fell on paths where it was stepped on and eaten by birds. Some seed fell on rocky ground and sprouted but had no earth to cling to and no moisture, and in the hot sun was scorched and withered. Some seed fell on thorny ground and the thorns sprang up with the seed and choked it. But some fell into good ground and grew and produced fruit. Sow goodness and some will sprout.

The Kingdom of Heaven is like a field worker who sowed seed in a field. While the worker slept the wheat sprang up but so did tares and weeds. The worker went to the owner of the field, saying, 'I planted good seed so where did these tares and weeds come from? Should I go and pick out the weeds?'

The owner replied, 'The good and the evil grow up together, intertwined. Leave the tares alone so you don't pull up the wheat. Let both grow together until the harvest, then the tares and wheat will be separated. Then the bad will be done away with and the good will be reaped.' Do not lose sight of goodness by being worried about the weeds.

The one who searches will find. The one who has will have more.

The Kingdom of God is enlightenment, like a man who cast a seed into his garden. And at night as he slept and during the day as he worked, that seed grew into a plant. That man didn't truly know how that plant grew. The earth brings life and the plant grew into a large tree with thick branches for the birds to perch on. And on the branches grew fruit which were picked in the harvest. The harvest is not at some far off time or when death steals in like a thief, but the harvest is very soon, now.

The Kingdom of God is like a bit of yeast which a woman kneads into her dough until the whole rises.

Enlightenment is like treasure a man finds buried in a field. The man is so full of joy he goes and sells all that he has and buys the field.

The Spirit of God is like a merchant who seeks good pearls, and when he finds one very beautiful pearl, sells all that he has to buy it.

Every person who knows the Kingdom of Heaven is like a householder who brings out his treasures new and old. One truth does not negate another.

The Kingdom of Heaven is like a farmer who went out early in the morning to hire laborers to work in his vineyard. When he agreed with the laborers on one coin a day they began working. Later the farmer saw others in the market looking for work. He said to them, 'You can have a job working in my vineyard and I'll pay you fairly.' They accepted. At noon and then again in the afternoon the farmer hired workers for his vineyard.

In the evening he went out and found others standing on the street and said to them, 'Why do you stand here all day doing nothing?'

They responded, 'Because no one has hired us.' The farmer hired them also, promising them a fair wage.

At the end of the day, as the sun was reddening the sky, the Lord of the vineyard called the laborers to gather so he could pay them their wages. First he paid those hired in the evening, giving each a coin. Those hired early in the morning therefore expected to receive much more, but were given one coin each. They said to the farmer, 'They've only worked an hour and you paid them the same as us. We've worked the whole day in the sun.'

The farmer answered, 'Friend, I do you no wrong. Didn't you agree to work all day for one coin? Can't I do what I want with my own money? Are you mad because I'm generous?'

As Jesus spoke a woman lifted up her voice saying, "Blessed is the womb from which you were born and the breasts that nursed you."

Jesus replied, "Yes, and blessed are all who hear God and obey. Anyone who acts with God is my brother and sister and mother."

Jesus knew humanity. He knew what was in their hearts and in their minds.

In the evening Jesus called his disciples to him and said, "I have compassion for these people. They've been here with me for three days now and there's no food for them. We need to feed them." Jesus asked the disciples to gather what food there was in the crowd. They gathered seven barley loaves and two fish.

Jesus bid the people to sit there in the field and then took the loaves and fish and, looking up to the heavens, gave thanks, blessed and broke the food, and gave it to his disciples who helped pass it out. It was served, and all ate.

Jesus spoke, "You ate of the loaves and were filled. Don't work for what is here today and gone tomorrow, but for that which endures forever. To do God's work you must believe in the Messiah."

God gives bread from Heaven to eat. The bread of God is he who comes from God and gives life to the world. The Messiah is the bread of life. The one who walks the way of the Messiah won't hunger and the one who believes won't thirst. All that God gives comes through the Messiah, his way, what he is. Everyone who sees the Son of God will have life. He who is of God knows God. He who believes in God has life. Christ is the living bread which comes from God. Whoever eats the flesh and drinks the blood will have life, and will dwell in God, and God in him.

From that time on many followers went back and followed Jesus no more.

While Jesus was praying with his disciples he asked them, "Will any of you leave also?"

Peter answered, "Where would we go?"

Jesus then asked, "Who do people say I am?"

They replied, "Some say John the Baptist. Or one of the prophets."

"Yes, and who do you say I am?"

Peter answered, "You are Christ, the Son of God. Your path is our path, the path of humanity. Your way is salvation and redemption."

"You're blessed Peter because God has shown you this. It is on your rock that my church will be built."

Jesus began telling his disciples, "I must go to Jerusalem, be rejected by the teachers of the law, suffer, be killed, and on the third day be raised again."

The disciples grew sad. Peter began to rebuke Jesus, saying, "Don't say that. That can't happen."

Jesus responded, "Place your life upon God's altar and receive your life. Whoever saves their life will lose it and whoever will lose their life for God will find it. What if a man gains the whole world and loses his life? What would a man give in exchange for his life? You will see God. God will reward each according to his works. You will know Messiah. You will establish God's Kingdom."

James asked Jesus, "Teacher, what is the soul?"

Jesus responded, "Where can the line be drawn between one's spirit and the Holy Ghost? God is the Great Spirit and all-encompassing power. God is the soul. Man is a microcosm. Every soul is divine."

But James was confused by this answer. "If every soul is divine then is there a hell?"

Jesus answered, "Who believes my words? Sin is the slave master, and is Hell. If one truly knew how sacred existence is then they truly would be. If they truly knew that their own life's journey is the journey of all of existence. If they knew that the world is filled with spirits that must be honored and celebrated. The truth will set you free."

James said, "We are not slaves. We do not need to be set free."

Jesus answered, "Whoever sins is the slave of sin."

James and John asked Jesus, "Please, let us sit with you in your kingdom, one on your right side and the other on your left."

The other disciples heard the request of James and John and became angry.

Jesus spoke to them, "The kingdom is for those with God. If I honor myself my honor is nothing. It is God that honors me. The princes of this world exercise dominion over all, and those who are powerful exercise authority by them and over them. It won't be this way with you. Whoever will be great among you must be a servant. Humans are on earth to help each other, and to give their lives to free others. Do not be self-serving."

The disciples asked Jesus, "Who is the greatest in the Kingdom of Heaven?"

Jesus called a little child to him and said, "Unless you become like a little child you will not establish the Kingdom of Heaven. Whoever humbles himself as this little child is the greatest in Heaven. If anyone wants to be first he must be last and be a servant to all.

I thank you God because these things are hidden to the wise and prudent, but revealed to babies. This is as it should be. All is delivered from God to the child of God. No one knows God but the child of God. No one is a child of God that does not know God.

Come to God all who labor and are laden with cares, and rest. Learn of the way of Christ Messiah, for I am meek and humble, and your soul will find rest. My burden is light.

If a man has a hundred sheep and one gets lost, won't he leave the ninety nine and go to seek the stray one? And when he finds it he calls together his friends and neighbors saying, 'Rejoice with me.' He rejoices more because of that sheep than he ever did over the ninety nine. In the same way Heaven will rejoice over one sinner who repents, more than over ninety nine just people who never repent.

If a woman has ten silver coins and loses one, she will light a candle, sweep the house, and search carefully till she finds it. And when she finds it she will call her friends and neighbors together, saying, 'Rejoice with me.' In the same way there's joy before God over one who repents.

A man had two sons. The youngest said to his father, 'Give me my inheritance now.' And the father did. The young man then packed and left his father's house and went to a far-off city where he lived easily and did what he pleased. When he had spent all of his money there were hard times in that city and he was soon impoverished and hungry. The young man worked feeding pigs but still was so hungry that he secretly ate from the pigs' food. Then he said to himself, 'My father has workers that are fed. I'll go to him and ask to work as a servant.'

The young man began the journey home and when he was still far out in the fields his father saw him and ran out to greet him, hugging and kissing him. The son said, 'Father, I've been wrong. I've been a bad man and a bad son. I'm not worthy to be your son.'

But the father bid his son to change into good clothes, and asked his servants to kill the fattened calf, and planned a feast.

The man's older son had been out in the fields, and as he came home he heard music and saw dancing. He asked one of the workers what was going on and was told, 'Your brother has come home and your father is celebrating his safe return.' The brother was angry and wouldn't go into the house for fear of becoming violent. Soon his father came out and found him and asked him to come inside.

The son said, 'Father, I've been a good son to you all these years. I've been loyal and honest to you. But I've never had a party. As soon as this bum who has spent all your money on prostitutes and drugs comes home you kill the fattened calf and there's a big celebration.'

The father answered, 'Son, you've always been with me and all that I have is yours. It's right that we should celebrate your brother's return because he was dead but now is alive, he was lost and now is found.'"

Jesus received word from Mary and Martha that their brother Lazarus was sick. Jesus travelled to Bethany to be with them.

When Jesus and his followers came to Bethany they found that Lazarus had been dead and buried for four days. Martha went out to meet Jesus on the road while Mary remained in the house sitting quietly.

Lazarus was the only son of a widow. The widow was there with many others, and she was distraught.

When Mary saw Jesus she rose hastily and went to him and began to cry. When Jesus saw her weeping he groaned in his heart and was troubled. Jesus had compassion for the women and said, "Don't cry. Where have you laid him?"

Martha replied, "I will take you there."

Jesus cried. Many there thought, 'He must have loved Lazarus very much.'

The grave of Lazarus was a cave with a stone over it. Jesus asked for the stone to be removed. Martha said, "He has been dead for four days."

Another said to Jesus quietly, "It will stink."

"You will see the glory of God. The power of death will be overcome. Lazarus will conquer death."

The stone was removed from the grave. Jesus lifted his eyes to the sky and said, "God, I thank you. I know you always hear me, when words are spoken and when they are not." Jesus then called with a loud voice, "Lazarus, rise up and come out."

And Lazarus came up out of the grave bound in grave cloth and his face behind cloth. His mother ran to hold him.

A fear gripped the people there and they knew that they were in the presence of a great prophet, and in the presence of God. The leaders of the town came and told Jesus and his followers to leave.

James grew angry and said, "I hope this town burns."

Jesus said to him, "That is in the spirit of hatred. Humans are not here to destroy but to save."

They moved on.

On the road to Jerusalem Jesus spoke to the twelve disciples, "We go to Jerusalem where I will be condemned to death. I will be laughed at, spit on, whipped, and crucified. On the third day I will rise again."

Jesus and the disciples passed by a man, named Bartimaeus, who had been born blind. Bartimaeus, when he heard from the crowds that Jesus was passing by, began to cry out, saying, "Jesus, son of King David, have mercy on me." Many told him to be quiet, but he yelled louder, "You are the son of King David, show me mercy."

Jesus asked the blind man, "What is it you want me to do for you?"

"I want you to give me my sight."

The disciples asked Jesus, "Is this man blind because of his own sin or because of the sin of his parents?"

Jesus answered, "Neither. This man is as he is so that the works of God are made manifest in him."

Jesus took Bartimaeus and washed his face and eyes with his tears, and the man could then see bright yellow light and truly saw and followed Jesus in the way.

Neighbors and those who had seen Bartimaeus begging when he was blind, said, "This man is now different."

Some said to the man, "How were your eyes opened?"

"A man named Jesus washed the dirt from my eyes and I received sight."

They then asked him, "Where is this Jesus?" But he didn't know.

Bartimaeus was brought before the teachers of the law. He was asked how he had received his sight. He responded, "A man named Jesus washed the dirt from my eyes and I received my sight."

"And on what day was this done?"

"On the holy day."

Some of the teachers said, "This Jesus is not of God because he doesn't keep the Sabbath holy."

Others said, "How can a man do such miracles if he is not of God?"

They asked Bartimaeus, "What do you say about this Jesus?"

"He is a prophet."

Those against Jesus said, "No, he is a sinner."

"I don't know if he is a sinner or not, but one thing I do know: I used to be blind but now I see."

"How did he open your eyes?"

"I've already told you and you didn't hear. Why should I tell you again? Will you become his followers?"

"You are his follower but we follow Moses. We know God spoke to Moses, but this Jesus? We know nothing about him."

"And if Moses were here right now, what would you say of him? That you do not know him because he is not Abraham? Would you be plotting his destruction because his ways are new? The man named Jesus has opened my eyes. How can God not be with him?"

They answered, "You were born in sin and you think you can teach us?" And they cast Bartimaeus out of the community.

As Jesus and his followers approached Jerusalem and came to the Mount of Olives, two disciples borrowed a young donkey for Jesus to ride on.

A great crowd spread palm fronds on the road, lining the way into Jerusalem. They called, "Blessed is the King who comes in the highest." All of Jerusalem was energized with the news of the coming of Jesus of Nazareth the prophet.

Jesus was surrounded by children and the disciples began to scold them and chase them away. Jesus said, "Don't be annoyed by children because they are the Kingdom of God. Whoever receives a child receives God. Whoever does not receive God as a little child will not be with God. We must save that which is lost to us."

In the sheep market was a pool called Bethesda. In and around the pool lay the sick, waiting for the water to be stirred up by God and become healing water. This was a firmly held belief for which many came to the pool. One man there had been unable to walk for thirty-eight years and his body was thin and weak.

Jesus asked him, "Do you want to be healed?"

The man replied, "There is no one to put me in the water when it is touched by God. Others step in before me and crowd me out."

Jesus said, "Rise, pick up your bed, and walk. The water of life flows from God."

Immediately the man was whole and picked up his bedding and walked. This occurred on a holy day. Soon the man was questioned why he carried his bedding on the holy day which was illegal to do. The man responded, "The one who healed me told me to pick up my bed and walk."

A teacher of the law then asked, "Who told you this?"

The man looked to see Jesus but could not find him in the crowd.

Later Jesus came to the man in the temple and they spoke together. The man learned Jesus' name and later told many who it was who had healed him. Teachers of the law heard of this and knew Jesus had healed on the holy day.

The teachers of the law then went to Jesus, accusing him of not keeping the Sabbath holy. Jesus replied, "Our Father works so I must work. You honor God with your lips but your hearts are far from God. You worship in vain. You teach doctrines but you go against God and to go against God is to lose yourself, your spirit. Religion is not a strange ideology to believe or not believe, but is self-evident truth."

Jesus went to the temple. He saw all who sold and bought in the temple, the moneychangers and those who sold oxen, sheep, and doves.

"My house will be a house of prayer, not a den of thieves. Look at this great and beautiful temple. The day will come when there will not be one stone left on top of another. All will be thrown down."

Some came to him and asked, "Then how should the temple be?"

Jesus answered, "The temple must be a sanctuary, a sacred place, where money, sin, blame, and evil are not discussed. Only devotion. It must be a place of reverence, a place of prayer. It must never be locked. The temple must be filled with sacred art, candlelight, and incense. A quiet place. But do not forget that each of you are a temple, a temple to God, with devotion in the heart, devotion of the spirit. And in this way you will build a temple of this world. This world is filled with hate, fear, greed, and lies. Be a temple to existence, full of peace and love, bravery and honesty."

Jesus, early in the morning, went to the temple to sit and to teach. Teachers of the law brought a woman to Jesus and said to him, "This woman was found in the act of adultery. Our law says she must be stoned to death. What do you think?"

Jesus bent down and wrote with his finger in the dust. When the question was asked of him again he stood and said, "He who is sinless should throw the first stone." Then he squatted and continued writing in the dust. Those who had heard him were convicted by their own consciences, and began leaving, one by one, quietly, the older ones first. Jesus and the woman were left there alone. Jesus said to her, "Where are your accusers? No one condemns you?"

"No one, sir."

"I don't condemn you either. Go and sin no more."

Jesus went to the Festival of Shelters. Teachers of the law sought him there. There was murmuring at the festival, some saying Jesus was a good man, others that he was a trickster. No one spoke openly because of fear of the authorities. During the festival Jesus went into the temple and taught.

Jesus said, "The one who follows me will not walk in darkness but will have the light of life. This doctrine isn't mine, but God's. It is known by anyone who knows God. Do not judge by appearances, but judge rightly.

Each receives their own light. Make your light to shine brightly. Be positive. No two people are the same so that, together, humans may succeed, physically, mentally, and spiritually. To hide one's gifts, to hate one's self, or another, is hatred of God, our Father."

One asked, "Where is your father? Why doesn't he come down here?"

Jesus replied, "You will never know God if you say God is a man you've never met. When in fact God has been all around you your entire life. You will never know me because you say God cannot be a man. You do not know me, my way, nor God, because you say God cannot be. Yet I say you cannot be, because what cannot be God?

Two men went into the temple to pray, one a teacher of the law and the other a commoner. The teacher stood and prayed, thanking God that he was a just man, not an adulterer, and not like the commoners nearby. The man said to himself, 'I fast twice a week, I give tithes weekly. I am such a good man for being of my religion. Oh, God, give me what I want.' Meanwhile the other man prayed on his knees far off in the corner of the temple, quietly yearning for God. And this man, not the teacher, found God.

The stone which the builders rejected has become the cornerstone, as was the fate of God, and it is marvelous in our eyes.

When you are invited to a wedding don't sit in a place of honor because the host may come and ask you to move and you will be shamed. Sit in the lowest place so that when the host sees you there he will ask you to move forward to a place of honor. Whoever exalts himself will be made a fool and whoever humbles himself will be honored.

Do not be as worried about recompense and pay-back as in doing the right thing. When you plan a feast do not think only of your friends, family, and neighbors, and those who are powerful and have authority over you. Call also the poor and the ill. By this you will be just and blessed.

A rich man planned a great feast and invited many. When the fattened calves and lambs had been butchered and all was prepared, he sent his servants to say to those invited, 'Come. All is ready.'

But the guests each made excuses, one saying, 'I'm in the midst of buying land and must finish my business.' Another said, 'Please excuse me. I'd like to come but my wife makes it impossible.'

The master became angry and told his servants to go into the streets of the city and invite the poor, the maimed, and the blind. 'Fill my house,' he instructed. 'None who were invited will taste this feast.'

I was hungry and you gave me food. I was thirsty and you gave me water. I was a stranger and you sheltered me. I was naked and you clothed me. I was sick and you cared for me. I was in prison and you visited me. As you have done these things for the least of my brothers and sisters you have done them for me, for Christ, for God, for humanity, for your soul.

All is change, all is permanence. All is distinct, and all is one. Out of one comes many and out of many comes one. All the Universe, all the mind, is of God. All is interrelated.

Do not fill your heart with worries. Do not let your life slip away.

My way is to become God. Whoever follows my way is a creature of light. I didn't come to judge the world but to save the world. God's covenant is Life."

Many did not believe in the Messiah's true nature because their eyes were blind and their hearts cold and hard. They were unable to understand with their hearts. Many felt the power of God but denied it because they were scared others might call them fools for speaking in a different way.

Jesus walked in the cloister attached to the temple. Some men came to him and told him sternly, "If you're the Christ tell us."

Jesus answered, "The works that I do in God's name bear witness to who I am. But you do not believe me. Those who know my way have conquered death. They are with God, and are God, as I am one with God."

Some picked up rocks to stone Jesus. Jesus answered their actions, "I have done many good acts for God. For which one do you stone me?"

"We stone you for your words of blasphemy. Because you are a man but you call yourself God."

"It is written in Psalms, 'You are gods. You are all sons of the Most High.' Well, what do you think this means? So do I blaspheme if I say I am the Son of God, or my followers are true children of God, or that you are God, though you do not know it and will not be fulfilled by it?

If you cannot believe in me or my way, believe in the good works I do. Aren't the hungry fed, the naked clothed, the homeless sheltered, the sick cared for, the dead respected, lovers married, children cared for, and the future of all protected? Know that God is in me and I am in God and my way is open to all. If some do evil in God's name, then you do good.

A man had two sons. He said to the first, 'Go work today in the vineyard.' The son answered, 'I will not.' But later that son repented and went and worked in the fields.

The man told his second son to go and work in the vineyard. The son responded, 'I will.' But he did not. So which son did what his father wanted?"

The men responded, "The first son."

"In the same way many criminals and homeless and those of diverse beliefs will know God before the teachers of the law. John came in righteousness and the teachers didn't believe, but many others did believe, people who are called common and scum. Most deny the obvious sign of holiness if it is outside their circle."

A man came to Jesus and asked, "Moses said that if a man dies having had no children his brother will marry his wife so that she may become pregnant. But what if there were seven brothers and the first married and before he could have children he died, so the wife then married the second brother who also died, and on and on until the woman had married all seven in turn. So whose wife will she be in Heaven?"

Jesus answered, "Do you think God is a man with human thoughts who lives in a nice place called Heaven? There is no marriage in Heaven. Time and space are the walls of reality. Beyond this reality are the eternity and infinity of Heaven. The timelessness. God is Heaven, therefore Heaven is here and now if one would only see it. God is not the God of the dead, but of the living. Neither God nor the dead are in a magical place but are in all places."

A man asked Jesus, "Which is the greatest commandment in the law?"

Jesus responded, "You will love God with all your heart and with all of your soul, and with all your mind. This is the first and greatest commandment, and the second is the same as the first: love others and love yourself. In fact, hold a deep-seated respect and love for all. God is love. These two commandments encompass all the law."

The man said, "I see the truth of it."

"You are not far from the Kingdom of God." Then Jesus told this story, "A man was travelling from Jerusalem to Jericho and was attacked by thieves who beat and cut him and stole his money, jewelry, even his clothes, and left him near death. A bishop came near and when he saw the wounded man passed by on the other side of the road. Similarly a rich man passed and came and looked at the hurt man, but did not want to become involved. Then a poor immigrant saw the wounded man and had compassion. He cleaned the man's wounds and dressed them and rode the man on his donkey to his house where he continued to care for the stranger. That man spent all his money serving his fellow human. Whoever gives a cup of cold water to one in need receives God. Go, and show mercy like this."

A young girl invited Jesus to come eat dinner with her family. Though she did not show signs of disease her family was disfigured by leprosy and lived in a leper colony outside Jerusalem. She was too young to know that she shouldn't invite Jesus to dinner.

After dinner Jesus and the young girl sat outside the tents staring up at the night's sky.

"Teacher, how many stars are there?"

"More than you could count if you spent your whole life counting."

"But how long will I live?"

"A very long time."

"But how many years have the stars been there?"

"More years than you could count if you spent your whole life counting."

"Did God create the sky?"

"God is creation. God is creating the sky now."

Jesus sat on the Mount of Olives. His followers came to him asking when the world would end.

Jesus answered, "The Kingdom of God will not come in the sky but is within you.

There will be betrayal and hatred. There will be no justice and love will turn cold. The brother may betray his brother, and the father may rape his own child, and children may murder their own parents. All sorts of terrible things may happen in this world, but endure. You will hear of wars and rumors of wars. Nation will rise against nation. There will be famines and disease and earthquakes will shake the ground. All these things will be full of sadness, but endure. Such things are facts and must come to pass. But they will not be the end of this world.

Go and preach, saying, 'the Kingdom of Heaven is here and now.' Heal the sick, raise the dead, cast out devils.

Give freely as you have received. Carry no money nor clothing. You will be fed. When you stay in a house let your peace be on that house. Whoever receives you receives God. And whoever does not receive you and shows you no hospitality, shake the dust off your sandals and move on.

Beware of lies which are always growing. I send you as sheep to the wolves, so be wise but be harmless. You must have strength, courage, bravery. When you find true being with God you will have these things in abundance. Endure and be a witness to goodness, a light to all people. In your endurance you will keep your soul. You will be brought before judges and governors because you speak against what they do. Do not worry about your defense, but go to court and speak the words in your heart. The Spirit of God will speak through you.

You will be persecuted in one city, then flee to another. All of you will suffer, and will be hated, and beaten, and may be killed for doing good. Don't fear the killers of this world, but fear the loss of your soul. It can be lost.

No one knows the day and hour. Two men will be in the field and one will be taken and the other left behind. Two women will be grinding at the mill and one will be taken and the other left. Be on the lookout because you do not know when death will come. Know that when you say goodbye to your loved ones that you may never see them again. Before history people ate and drank, they traded goods, they planted, they built, they married, babies were born, and people died. Death is part of the journey of life. Hold no regret towards life. When one dies one is dispersed out into the Universe, to be part of all. God is all.

There is nothing covered that won't be revealed, nothing hidden that won't be known. What is said in darkness will be repeated in the light.

Many false prophets will come, saying, 'I speak for God,' but know that God speaks within you. The teachers of the law are hypocrites. They put heavy burdens on people's backs and offer no help to lighten the load. They want only to look good in the eyes of others. They love to be in positions of honor and to be greeted with titles of respect. They love to speak but they say little.

The teachers of the law are sure to make the outside of their bodies clean, while the insides are decay. They consider money above all else, and ignore the love of God. They are like painted tombs, which appear to be beautiful but are full of putrid death. They appear righteous but are corrupt.

It is these people who kill the prophets and then bury them in golden sepulchers. But this is the way of it, prophets are persecuted and murdered, their blood has been shed since the foundation of the world. But this does not vindicate the teachers of the law. They refuse knowledge and hide the keys so that others may not have it either. They are full of hate for those they deem weak and inferior. And does their hate for others cause them to hate themselves any less? Their sin is impurity, an irreverence towards the holy, a deep-seated irreverence.

The one who is greatest among you serves the others. You are all brothers and sisters. You are all children of God. Whoever humbles himself will be exalted in spirit."

John spoke, "We saw a man casting out demons in your name, a man we had never seen before. We stopped him."

Jesus replied, "Do not stop him because the one that is not against us is with us. Know respect and tolerance. I want the unity of all people and of all my followers, in their hearts and minds. I do not want an end to distinct peoples, but a co-being. God has given us a wide variety of creation, and this world requires all of that variety.

Blessed is that servant, the faithful and wise steward."

The teachers of the law gathered at the palace of the high priest Caiaphas. They discussed what should be done about Jesus. Caiaphas argued, "If we do nothing we show our support for him. The Romans will see this as rebellion and will march on Jerusalem."

An army officer said, "No man has ever spoken like this Jesus."

A minister spoke, "Are you also deceived? These common people who believe him are fooled and are cursed."

The priest Nicodemus spoke up, "Does our law judge any man before he is heard and a case against him is constructed?"

Another responded, "Are you from Galilee also? No prophet comes from there."

They decided that nothing should be done during the Passover because it might cause the people to rise.

Simon the Patriot came to Jesus. He had been a soldier, a guard at the temple. "Teacher, I know this high priest Caiaphas. He has gone to great pains to hide the fact that his son was caught on the temple grounds with a prostitute. Let us blackmail Caiaphas because this news, if released, would destroy him."

Jesus responded, "Do you truly know this man? Or his son? And why have you not told this information earlier? Is it because you do not fully believe it or because you know it would destroy Caiaphas and his son?"

"But teacher, shouldn't such a dark crime be revealed, and punished properly?"

"Simon, I know you can forgive your comrades and yourself, but can you forgive a stranger?"

Jesus told Peter and John, "Find a large furnished upper room where we may eat the Passover Feast."

In the evening Jesus came with his twelve apostles and gathered with many who were not loved by others, criminals, prostitutes, and the very poor. As they gathered Jesus said, "Peace be with you."

Jesus sat at the table with all. Lazarus was there. The food was served by Martha.

Jesus said, "Brothers and sisters, you saw the lambs sacrificed today. Life must be taken with reverence. Hold gratitude for the sacrifice. Be humble and perform selfless acts and you will be as a sacrifice to God. Go and find out what it means that God wants mercy, not animal sacrifices."

Then Mary wept at Jesus' feet and wiped them with her hair and kissed his feet and anointed his feet and head with perfume and oil, and wiped his feet with her long hair. The house was filled with the scent.

Jesus rose from the table, stripped to the waist, and took a towel and poured water into a basin and began to wash his followers' hands, heads, and feet, and to wipe them with the towel.

"The one who is a servant of others receives God. The leaders of this world rule over the people and are called benefactors. But you shouldn't seek power like this. You must be a servant to others. I appoint you leaders of a kingdom, the Kingdom of God, the Kingdom of the Spirit. It is here, now, in your heart. You will feast at God's table like kings."

As they sat and ate Jesus said, "My time is at hand. I've desired to eat this dinner with you before I die. I won't eat again. This is our communion, our co-being, our unity, with all of existence, with each other, with God."

Then he took bread and gave thanks and broke it, and gave it to the disciples, saying, "This is my body which is given to you."

He took the cup and gave thanks and said, "Take this and drink. This cup is God's covenant, my blood shed for you, for the forgiveness of sins."

Jesus poured a libation onto the ground to honor the dead.

"Now humanity is glorified and God glorified through humanity. I will be with you a little longer. A new covenant and a new commandment I give you: peace and love. This is my way.

Don't be troubled. As you know God you know me. I will come again and again, until you know my way. I am the way, the way of truth, awakening, and life.   If you know me you know God. I am humanity and God, sacrificed for humanity and for God.

God is never hidden from you unless you do not open your eyes. The Spirit of God is in you. In spirit there is nothing you cannot know, cannot feel. Remember love.

Peace I leave with you, my peace I give to you. Don't have a troubled heart. Do not be afraid.

I am never separated from God, nor will I be in death.

As we are Messiah, we are God. Bear fruit. Cut away every branch that doesn't bear fruit. Live in my love. Be full of joy. Love one another as I have loved you. No one has greater love than the one who lays down his life for his friends.

The world may hate you. My way is not always the easy way. You may be persecuted as the prophets were. Some will even kill in my name, thinking they do God's service. But know that my way is one of peace.

God will show you all things through the Holy Spirit.

Your sorrow will be turned into joy, your heart will rejoice."

Jesus, Peter, James, John, and Simon went to a garden called Gethsemane, through which a creek ran. Jesus became very sad and weighed down. "My soul is full of sorrow. Wait for me."

Jesus went off alone, fell, lay prone and prayed, saying, "God, I do not want to die. But I will not hide from what must be. Why does time go by so fast?" Jesus looked into the sky, lit by moonlight. The Spirit of God strengthened him.

Jesus prayed with all of his existence, until his sweat fell on the ground. He began to cry and took on the sin of the world. Jesus then became calm, praying and meditating for many hours.

A large group with torches and weapons entered the garden. They had been sent by the teachers of the law to arrest Jesus. Simon the Patriot drew his knife and stabbed one of the men, a guard named Malchus. Then Jesus spoke, "Put your weapon away. Whoever lives by the sword dies by the sword." Jesus healed the cut on Malchus' belly.

"I am Jesus of Nazareth. I'm the one you want. Why do you come out to arrest me at night with weapons? I have been sitting in the temple day after day and no one has tried to arrest me. This is the power of darkness."

Jesus' hands were tied with rope and a bag was put on his head. His guards hit him, saying, "Prophesy for us. Who hit you?" and laughed.

Jesus was led to where Caiaphas the high priest and the teachers of the law were assembled. Witnesses against Jesus presented themselves to the council, including the apostle Judas Iscariot.

A witness stated, "This man said, 'I am able to destroy the temple of God.'"

The high priest turned to Jesus. "How do you answer that?"

Jesus said nothing.

Caiaphas continued, "Tell us, are you the Christ, the Son of God?"

"I am."

Caiaphas yelled, "He has spoken blasphemy. We need no more witnesses."

Many in the council hollered out, "He is guilty."

Some spat on Jesus and some hit him.

Caiaphas then asked Jesus about his doctrines and disciples, to which Jesus answered, "I spoke openly to the world. I taught in public and hid nothing. My teaching is known to many. Ask them."

A soldier standing near Jesus hit him in the head, saying, "You speak to the high priest with respect."

The next morning Jesus was bound and led to the courts and presented to Governor Pontius Pilate.

The teachers of the law accused Jesus, "He stirs up hatred among the people against the Empire. He tells them that paying taxes is illegal and that he himself is the king of the Jews."

Pilate then asked Jesus, "Are you the king of the Jews?"

Jesus answered, "This is what the teachers of the law call me. My kingdom is not of this world, but of the Spirit."

"Then why do these men accuse you? Why do they want you dead?"

"Because I bear witness to the truth."

Pilate responded, "But what is the truth?"

"Truth is the authority of the universe. My truth is of the heart and of the spirit."

The teachers of the law accused Jesus of many things but Jesus did not say anything more.

Pilate asked him, "Why don't you speak and defend yourself?"

But Jesus continued to be quiet.

When Pilate discovered that Jesus was from Galilee he said, "This man is under Herod's jurisdiction." Jesus was then sent to Herod who was in Jerusalem at that time.

Herod was thankful to now meet him. He hoped to see Jesus perform a miracle. He asked many questions of Jesus, but when Jesus answered none of them, grew angry and began to mock him.

Herod's soldiers dressed Jesus in a blanket as a king's robe and called him "the king of shit." Jesus was then returned to Pilate's court.

On that day Herod and Pilate, who had been at odds with each other in the past, became friends.

Pilate presented Jesus alongside Barabbas to the crowds. Barabbas had committed murder during an insurrection against Rome.

Many in the crowd who considered themselves good people cried out for Jesus' death because his blasphemy was an affront to their religion, his peace was against their politics, and his love was against their sense of strength.

Pilate's wife pleaded with Pilate to have nothing to do with Jesus' punishment, knowing he was a just man.

Pilate responded, "It is out of my hands. There are laws in place. By making himself king he spoke against Caesar. I wash my hands of it."

Jesus was brought to the Praetorium, stripped naked by soldiers, and whipped until blood pooled on the tiles. A crown of thorns was forced onto Jesus' head and he was delivered to be crucified.

Jesus, bearing his cross, went to the place of skulls. Along the way he fell and a man named Simon was compelled by the soldiers to carry the cross. There followed a large group of people behind Jesus, crying, their spirits crushed.

At the place of skulls Jesus was nailed to the cross and crucified. By the cross stood the apostles, Mary his mother, Martha, Mary Magdalene, and the other disciples. Jesus called down, "Take care of my mother."

Jesus said, "God forgive them because they do not know what they are doing."

At the base of the cross was a large stone which, though it had never been hewn, was an altar. Two symbols were on the stone: ☼ ⊕, the Earth being God's altar.

Clouds filled the large sky, sunlight streaking through, and darkness then came over the land. Jesus cried loudly, "My God, my God, why have you forsaken me?" He then gave up his spirit. The veil of the temple ripped in two from top to bottom. Wind, thunder, and rain. The earth quaked.

His sacrifice brings forgiveness and perfect freedom.

Many who saw him die said, "This was a righteous man." Many followers, men and women alike, beheld these things.

When the soldiers came to Jesus they saw that he was dead. One of the soldiers pierced his side with a spear.

When the evening came Joseph, a disciple of Jesus, went to the Praetorium and asked for Jesus' body. Joseph and others took the body down from the cross and wrapped it in a clean linen cloth with myrrh and aloes. Jesus' body was then laid in a tomb cut into rock within the garden of Gethsemane. A large stone was placed across the entrance of the sepulcher.

Three days after Jesus' death Mary Magdalene and Martha went to the garden in which he was buried. It was early in the morning. They brought incense to the tomb. When they arrived they found that the large stone which had covered the entrance had been rolled away. Mary entered the tomb slowly. All was still but for dust in the sunlight. She saw the burial linen before her. She then turned and saw a young man sitting on the right side. His clothes were white and light shone from him. "Do not be afraid. I know you seek Jesus. He is not here. He has risen."

Mary and Martha left the tomb with fear and joy and ran to tell the other disciples.

Jesus was seen, a figure of golden light on the shore.

Jesus is man, his Way open to all, and also God, the celestial priest, that which all yearn for.

There are many things Jesus did and said, so many that if they were all written down the world could not contain the books.

The end of this world is the beginning of the next. The end of this story is the beginning of a new one. Amen

www.ingramcontent.com/pod-product-compliance
Lightning Source LLC
Chambersburg PA
CBHW060040040426
42331CB00032B/1945

* 9 7 8 0 6 1 5 4 5 7 7 7 2 *